Carolina Ilica

Violet

Translators (from Romanian)
Olimpia Iacob and Jim Kacian; Lidia Vianu

Proverse Hong Kong
2019

Carolina Ilica • Violet

VIOLET is the expression of a woman seeking, achieving and deeply experiencing romantic and sensual love. The poems follow a similar trajectory to those of the English metaphysical poet John Donne and end with the persona equally intensely soliciting the embrace of God.

CAROLINA ILICA has been described as the most important Romanian woman poet of the second half of the Twentieth Century. Born in the village of Vidra, Vârfurile commune, Arad county, she graduated from the Faculty of Philosophy, University of Bucharest, in 1975. She is Vice-president and Artistic Director of the Foundation and Cultural Organisation, the International Academy Orient-Occident and Artistic director and Chairman of the Jury of the International Festival, Curtea de Argeş Poetry Nights. A member of several International Academies and Associations of Literature, Science and Arts, she is highly productive as translator, essayist, teacher, journalist and diplomat as well as with her poetic work. She was been awarded numerous national and international prizes.

VIOLET

CAROLINA ILICA

Proverse Hong Kong

Carolina Ilica ·Violet

Violet
by Carolina Ilica.
Copyright © Carolina Ilica April 2019
1st published in Hong Kong by Proverse Hong Kong,
April 2019 under sole and exclusive licence.
ISBN: 978-988-8491-43-8

Enquiries:
Proverse Hong Kong, P.O. Box 259, Tung Chung Post Office,
Tung Chung, Lantau Island, NT, Hong Kong SAR, China.
E: proverse@netvigator.com. W: www.proversepublishing.com

The right of Carolina Ilica to be identified as the author of this work
has been asserted by her
in accordance with the Copyright, Designs and Patents Act 1988.

Cover design by Artist Hong Kong.

All rights reserved. No part of this publication may be reproduced, stored in a retrieval system, or transmitted, in any form or by any means, electronic, mechanical, photocopying, recording or otherwise, without the prior written permission of the publisher or publisher and author. The book is sold subject to the condition that it shall not, by way of trade or otherwise, be lent, re-sold, hired out or otherwise circulated without the publisher's prior written consent in any form of binding or cover other than that in which it is published and without a similar condition including this condition being imposed on the subsequent owner or purchaser. Please contact Proverse Hong Kong in writing, to request any and all permissions (including but not restricted to republishing, inclusion in anthologies, translation, reading, performance and use as set pieces in examinations and festivals).

British Library Cataloguing in Publication Data.
A catalogue record for this book is available
from the British Library.

Carolina Ilica ·Violet

Motto

"If you want everybody to be crazy about you,
In velvet you will attire, my child, in black –
With your face as white as marble you emerge,
With your big eyes blazing in the vaults below your brow,
With fair bush-like hair, and shoulders white as snow –
In black, sweet mouth, you will look so well!
If you would please me, yes, me alone,
In violet-blue silk you will attire,
Its tinge of sweet, sweet bluish-grey (...)

Am I worthy of asking for, am I worthy of getting more?
Am I not listening to the slander around me any more?
Could I play the lyre to keep awake,
If not all the century, at least one hour, one day?
Such beautiful words have I tidied up in a string,
And spoken out what is on earth so dear to me, so sweet –
Is it the poet's mission, in the waves of his time,
                                                                                    to
deliver words,
To utter nonsense like bubbles of foam,
To gossip, to talk and talk
About how the moon comes out, and the wind blows

in the groves?
But no matter how much he may write or say ...
The forests, the fields, the plains can do it perfectly well,
They do it even better than how you say it in your lines.
Unlike that drawing too flat from modern lyrics,

Nature is loftier, loftier by far . . .
Oh, sad profession (. . .)

        (. . .) with me in a century for which
dreams and poetry are but a mere nothing."

From 'Icon and Frame' by **Mihai Eminescu**, 1876
Translated by Olimpia Iacob and Jim Kacian

Carolina Ilica •Violet

Dedication

I kiss the eyes of them that read
And kiss their eye-lashes indeed

And an eye-brow when they frown
If they think I'm here to moan

If the reader is a she
I will kiss her like a bee

If the reader is a he
I have kissed him already

And if it's a poet he
Let him kiss me, let him kiss me.

Carolina Ilica
(Translated by Olimpia Iacob and Jim Kacian)

VIOLET
CAROLİNA ILİCA

CONTENTS

Motto
From 'Icon and Frame' by **Mihai Eminescu,** 1876
Translated by Olimpia Iacob and Jim Kacian   5

Dedication by Carolina Ilica
Translated by Olimpia Iacob and Jim Kacian   7

I. LOVING IN SECRET (VIOLET)
Translated by
Olimpia Iacob and Jim Kacian

Violet Summer	15
Mulberries And Poppies	16
Small World	17
Hedonistic Summer	18
Whipping	20
I Want To See You Laugh	21
Machines	22
Beach	24
Tomorow Night	26
Addiction	28
Summer Nights	30
Shades	33
Magic Words	35
Jails	36
Serene	37
Intimacy	38
Portrait After Sleep	40
Waiting	41
After A Love Night	43
Afforestation	45
A Bed Too Narrow	49
Nausea	50
Abundance	51

Hat Veil	53
Absence	54
Promise	56
Moon	57
Dracula II	58
Torture	60
Quarrel	61
Delta	63
Ripe Fruits	64
Nocturnal Rain	66
Poetic Acuity	68
I Feel Like Crying	70
Red Apples (Dracula III)	72
Scraping Up Supper	74
Mourning	75
Self Portrait In Sleep	76

II. THE SHORT POEM OF MY LONG LIFE
13 (DOUBLE) POEMS OF LOVE
Translated by Lidia Vianu

1. a) Woodlander	78
2. b) Woodlander	79
2. a) Woodlander	80
2. b) A Dress	81
3. a) One Evening	82
3. b) Shameful	83
4. a) Dream	84
4. b) Temptation	85
5. a) He Was Caressing Me	86
5. b) Sleepless Nights	87
6. a) Nightflier	88
6. b) Nightflier	89

Carolina Ilica • Violet

7. a) Lakes	90
7. b) Lakes	91
8. a) "Calea Victoriei"	92
8. b) Love	93
9. a) Haystacks	94
9. b) Snails	95
10. a) Exquisitely	96
10. b) In Your Eyes	97
11. a) Out Of Fire And Ice	98
11. b) Summer Wanes	99
12. a) Evening-Plane	100
12. b) In Childhood (The Master Of The World)	101
13. a) The Short Poem Of My Long Life	102
13. b) Like A Peasant	103
The Translators	105
Response to the poet's work	106
Advance Responses to the English translation of *Violet*	107

I.

LOVING IN SECRET

Translated by
Olimpia Iacob and Jim Kacian

Carolina Ilica • Violet

Violet Summer

It's been so long since there was so violet a summer
May, that I am so deeply fond of, is in fashion again
With all its nuances
    shading off into pink or blue.

It's been so long since there was so exotic a summer
With so many landscapes
    and exotic fruit.
The ball of the mango seed
    is a fibrous lump
    cracking between the thighs
    of the yellow
    and so sweet-scented core
As a man's heart cracks
    for too much fullness.

It's been so long since there was so fatal a summer

So hard for you, for too much ease
So bad for me, for too much good.

Mulberries And Poppies

You have brought me the summer
With but a poppy.
Its tenderness
Is my tenderness, too:
    I fade away in only one life
    As much as it fades away in one day

The same day, walking
I picked for you
Purple mulberries almost ripe,
Thinking you also think
Of childhood.
Looked at from behind
Every childhood is like this:
    Happy, ah,
    And stained with mulberries!

So you have picked a poppy for me
I picked black mulberries for you
                  purple, in fact,
We have stolen
From no one,
    for each other.
The tender grass
        scant and short
Facing the town too high
Has grown tired of warmth and so much height.

Red and black. Black and red.
Sheer barter.
You took me to your mouth and I took you to my mouth.
Kissing me
      kissing you.
    Both kissing
O,
    Poetry
          my affective memory
Betrayed word for word!

Small World

How small the world is!
   I am
   Where you, too, once were.
   And you are
   Where I, too, once was.

I can imagine you
    going in and out
        out and in
            and again out
   From between the thighs of the seas:
      like a playful dolphin gliding into billows
      like a man
          having a woman
      like a successful swimmer
      streaming with water
          when ashore.

And if now I pass my tongue across my lips
I taste the sea's salt
   On my face?
   On your face?

I look forward to seeing you
              tasting you
Just as you taste
          some good purple wine
Before you enjoy it
And before him
   drunk
      drinks your mind.

Carolina Ilica • Violet

Hedonistic Summer

The pleasure of the new reading
      from Silva or Rojas
Is like love at first sight.
Of the resuming Yourcenar or Borges.
Of the long reciting Rilke.

And also other pleasures more carnal more mundane:
Swimming in the sea at night
         all naked
                  in the moonlight.

The lukewarm rain in the park
And the saliva on the leaves
Left by the snails
As if they advanced
      ever kissing.

The tiny balconies
Full of hydrangea
   hardly holding
      their head too big
Looking like vegetable brains
Pinkish, reddish-purple, bluish
Raising in one day
      as much as others in one year.
But greenish at first
Like some alien beings
   from the future.

The forest with umbelliferous shadows.
And the lake with the white water lilies.
   With clouds above
      and umbrellas:
         keeping off the sun? the rain?

Carolina Ilica •Violet

And
The others' memories –
    for one hundred years –
About Mihai Eminescu and
        Veronica Micle
  (The most praised Romanian female poet?)
She wearing a silk dress
    Rustling violet
And him in black
  putting on his top hat
    only to please her.

Sweet loving recurrent dusks
The midnights
    with you
From sweet to ever sweeter:
Like the core of the overripe fruit
Like the erotic rehearsal
From Maurice Ravel's Bolero.

You see
  she only remembers
    what she likes
This summer!

A summer
  also
    hedonistic!

Carolina Ilica • Violet

Whipping

His hair freshly cut, a man
    Smells fresh.
His hair cut short very short as if a soldier's haircut
Looking much younger
    Maybe for the sake of a woman
The park is hardly green.

I look for a hillock here
    a more swollen place
A moist heap of violets
    violet and suave (*Viola suavis*)
As I would be looking for your chest
    A pillow much harder
    To lay beneath the back of my head
    When I dream.

Then I look for two twin arms
Grown together
Of melancholic linden trees
Or maybe I look for your hands
To tie them together
    to seize them
And then to whip you
    with snaps of bloody twig
    ready-knotted here and there.

To whip you thoroughly
    so as to make you feel a bit of pain
        on the outside
    But as much as
You enjoy it the more.
As the longing
  Gives you pain
      on the inside.

Carolina Ilica • Violet

I Want To See You Laugh

I want to see you laugh
So that your eyes may catch fire
Devastating around
The violet groves
              Of dun-mauve dark rings
Of your nights hardly slept

I want to see you laugh
And me laugh with you again
    The upper teeth show themselves to the bottom ones
    And the bottom ones to the upper ones
    And yours to mine
    And mine to yours
    As the white pebbles on the two banks
        Sparkling at each other
    Come out from the violin-like water
    Of the rivers fled from the mountains

It is so much shared intimacy –
As if they made love again –
Among those who laugh together.

So let us scatter to the wind the preconceived idea
That poets have to be sad forever
And drink from The Holy Grail of sorrows!

They, too, are worthy to taste,
        to have at least an idea
        of what happiness looks like
If only for singing
        about it
                without it!

Carolina Ilica •Violet

Machines

A perfect machine
            for breathing,
Provided with a two-cycle engine
Self-adjusting
   raced throughout the day
   in slow-motion through the night,
Is your broad chest.

And my sleep near it is another
                     machine –
Provided with a balloon or wings
   for climbing, for dreaming? –
Able to rise ever higher
Till out of sight

      At a wedding in the skies
Where people drink red wine
Where
I also drink with pleasure
But my measure, velvet-like
                    and scarlet
     is hardly large as
Not even as big as the petal
Of the rose bush
          Baccara
That you always have with you.
   Indeed
your chest is a two-cycle engine
      breathing machine
         antiquity
               worn in and expensive
Working in the day time and in the night.
And my sleep
     A machine for air
Ever newer ever fragile
     With each night

Carolina Ilica • Violet

Hanging
   hanging
From the balloon blown up with the helium of dream
   much lighter than air
Or between the wings too large
   of a glider.

Ready to fall any time
To come down with a crash
   Without crushing
   But crashing you
      Against your chest.

Carolina Ilica • Violet

Beach

I keep basking in the sun.
My body all sweat beneath me
As if someone also were lying there
Makes my beach sheet wet.

My face gazes up between linden and birch
Abandoned beneath the cloud
That bends
      gray
As your hair once dark
Now fringed with silver.
   It gently bends
Over my fair face.

Seldom and barely perceptible
Pass by small planes
      of birds
Leaving behind a feather
That falls on the open book
By my head.
   At my head
      where
Like a cross in bloom
A shrub wild
      proud
Of hollyhock tall
      single
Swings its shoulders
With only one white-pink corolla on top:
Invaded by
Butterflies Polyommatus icarus
   Don Juans
      erotomaniac.

Carolina Ilica • Violet

I look at them
    but I forget them.
For in the lofty birch
Gentle
    little
        barely perceptible
Is the leaf light
As your sleep
    gentle
    and little
        barely perceptible:
Lying
In my involuntary
    memory
        indigo-violet.

Carolina Ilica • Violet

Tomorrow Night

There will be a full moon tomorrow night.
It will come into my house through the window
Like a lover obsolete and romantic
That won't let me sleep.
The full moon is strong as you are
And won't let me sleep.

It will definitely remind me of you:
    Standing
        like an everlasting Adam
In front of the open window
Drawing aside the curtain slightly.
Reaching out your arms even more
Drawing aside also
The outside curtain
        of the rain
Cold and with fringes

    Cooling you
        From me
            from yourself
                from both of us
After you've initiated me in wonders.
For wonders are those things that happen to you
For the first time!

Yes, there will be a full moon tomorrow night
And as it is now I shall have
        Bluish circles round my eyes.

But tomorrow there will be a full moon
And I will be having like now
                black and blue dark circles.
The full moon has your power
It doesn't let me sleep
Starting with this night
        when
I remember again:

Carolina Ilica • Violet

As you were standing
In front of the open window
Reaching out your arms
Slightly drawing aside
The other
      outside curtain
             of the rain
Cold
    with fringes.

While I kept praying
    deluding myself
Like Juliet
That that night,
    the first night,
Shall never meet the daybreak
    Never!

Carolina Ilica • Violet

Addiction

Like a drug addict
Drinking the hot smoke
    of marijuana
Or breathing in the pollen of cocaine
I have become.
Without needing
Anything of all that.
Except you
    but you
        again
   For you stir up my senses.
   You excite my mind.

To think no more of you
    I abandon myself to flowers
I keep gardening all day long.
My balcony is a home for flowers.
I talk to them I talk to each of them
I caress their leaves
   as if I caressed
      uncountable lips-
         that seem
            to all be yours!
Sometimes I sing for them.
The caresses stimulate their growth
   just as happens with babies.
My Japanese roses
   from several generations-
I am their mother, grandmother and great-grandmother –
Every day they show me one flower
   red, passionate
    and unique
      apparently useless
         But indispensable
Like beauty.
And Christmas Cactus – how do they count:
   using their fingers
      their blunt leaves

Carolina Ilica • Violet

      geometrically multiplied? –

Since they hang
Their cyclamen earrings
    right on Christmas!

But none of my flowers has a corolla
   violet
     or black.
None of them lets me think of you.
If I happen to think
   one thing or another
      drops out of my hand
I break everything in the house
For I am addicted to you

Dreaming of you
      over and
         over again
I drug myself with the violet
   nearly black
      (sedimented in my memory)

As if I drank the hot smoke
    of marijuana.
As if I breathed in the yellowish pollen
   of cocaine.

Carolina Ilica •Violet

Summer Nights

Summer nights when I sleep
As if in a native clearing
      refreshing myself
In the grass embellished with flowers of the bed sheets
With corollas of different shades of violet
Out of which I choose:
    Neither spring crocuses
        nor bluebells
           or sweet violets.

    Neither hollowworts
        nor pasque flowers.
    Neither acanthuses
        preciously speckled.
    Nor tiny calyces
        or tender foxgloves
    Spoilt with diminutives
        as children.
    Neither vulgar columbines
        also called the gypsy flower.
    Nor mulleins with spikes
        ever smaller and darker
            to their top
        as if they came to an end in the sky.
    Neither wild thyme
        lavender
            or healing
                mint.
Neither aconite
        tare
            Hungarian vetch
        in tendrils
            twining around
                the hayfield.

Carolina Ilica • Violet

Neither sage lamenting
Nor lilac (*Syringa vulgaris*)
Nor banewort
        a great lady
           Whose maiden name is *Atropa belladona*
Bearing on the same dress –
    as the Persimmon tree
        on the same branches –
Fruit and flowers at a time
(In a tiny dose
    Reassuring the heart)
(In a large dose
    Bringing death by poisoning).
Not even the thistles
    noble also
    but decayed now
    begging
    beside the edge of ditches
    or withdrawing far away
        in the mountains
        among cliffs solitary
        as hermits.

None of them.
Except
Only
    the irises being genuinely embarrassed for
The whiteness so white
Of the breasts.

I choose the irises
    with their stem long
        tremulous
Under the petals turned up and humid
        like a pair of labia.

Carolina Ilica • Violet

Summer nights
    when I am sleeping
                naked
On the irises violet and erotical
                of the bed sheets
Wakened up by the sun
Having dreams and dreaming myself
In the bottomless pit of your arms
    Under you
As under the fire sky,
    It also naked!

Carolina Ilica •Violet

Shades

I have ever worn shades of mauve as if in secret mourning
Ever awaiting you.
I wrote you poems
   long before
   we met.

When you read them
   And suddenly saw yourself in them
You were scared stiff!:
   As if about your own image come out at once
      multiplied
           and cast
As often
         and with all speed
By the windows of a long train whistling
When passing by your stopped train
But in the opposite direction.

Or about your own image
        repeatedly turned upside down
          trembling
            and drowned
In the mirrors ever deeper
      of the ever many other waters
      but belonging to the same river
Unwillingly floating to the other side
              of the world.

Now
    that we met
        is far more fatal
Than if we never met before.

Carolina Ilica • Violet

And all my old love poems
Have come to be
But shades of one poem
              violet.

But translatable periphrases
Of my LONGING
        Untranslatable.

Carolina Ilica • Violet

Magic Words

Eyes green
    poisonous
Eyes painful:
    Like those of the men after they have mixed
        their drinks
    Like those of the women in labor:
        With contractions ever swifter
            ever splitting
                ever more often
    As if they gave birth
        to other eyes:
            purplish.
Eyes green
    with poison
        poisonous
            as poison
Painful eyes:
    As if they had envenomed each other.
    As if the left eye
    Had bewitched
        the right eye.
    And the right eye
        the left.
Though they cannot see
        each other.
    Inaccessible
        to each other
As also the woman
    but only for a couple of days a month
    and only from waist to toes
        like a land mermaid
Becomes inaccessible to her man
They both feeling
    even more
    That they can touch completion
        only together.

Jails

Of all my black clothes
I would make a jail in mourning
To confine this night.

Of all my white clothes
I would make a bright jail
For who knows
       which day
Of our meeting again.

O,
   I wish
      I wish
There were no longer anything
Between this night
And that day!

   Except,
      maybe,
My iris-coloured dress
Falling off me
As the serpent in the Garden of Eden
After it had tempted.

Carolina Ilica • Violet

Serene

So serene is your sleep
That like a woman
After her first childbirth
I can be frightened
Not hearing
The serene breath
       too serene
            hardly perceptible
Of her baby
In the cradle.

Your cradle being my own breath.

So serene is your sleep
As if
   half of your breath
Were already
On the other
      violet bank
And only now and then
A gale brings with it
      But a mauve echo.

So serene is your sleep
And so scant the breath
In the room
As if one of us
        were dead
For so long waiting
    for the other.

Intimacy

It's endless, the lovers' caress,
Remember?
   She
   Dressed only in her own baby skin
   Nearly transparent
   Like a corolla of an apple blossom
   Through which one can see, indeed,
       violaceous venules
   Like some tiny flashes of lightning
       with no thunder
   But accompanied only by the tepid rain
       of the shower

Remember?
   She
   Like Mary from Magdala
   Washing both your feet
   With piety and worship
   One foot first
       then the other
               with no haste
   With sisterly affection at first
   And later on
   With quite dissolute lust
   To kiss
   Not your self-confident sole
   Or your nimble petulant
            heel
   But that white white hollow
   Untouchable when in motion
   By which the foot relaxes
   Pacing
   That pure nest
   Hermetic
   As the pubis of a little girl.

Carolina Ilica • Violet

Remember?
Of course, you do!
She kissing you
Where
      no one else
           had ever kissed you
And where
   no one else
      will ever
         kiss you!

Portrait After Sleep

A little girl waking up at the break of day
Sweaty in her sleep
                as flowers
When their armpits drip dew
It is morning in June.
Still unaware of her beauty.

She grows up as you are watching.
Your eyes caressing her
As you stand before the open window
    smoking and dreaming
    dreaming and smoking
With a total inner freedom
Which dream alone may give us.

A nimble teenager
        fussy
                and aware of
Her own beauty
The morning has become.
She tries on all the colours
Found in the wardrobe of the white light
Prone
    to choosing
        violet
Or, maybe, being chosen by it.

And here she is
        like an angel and a demon
Raising her look
    diverting it from her dream
        into your eyes.
And it's not you who will turn her
Or her sisters into a woman.
But maybe your offspring:
That volume of love poems
    made
        with several women.

Carolina Ilica • Violet

Waiting

My hair follows you.
It climbs up your right shoulder,
It chooses its parting itself
    Splitting in two
    Like a snake's tongue.
It then goes stealthily beneath your armpits
    Smelling of warm spices
    Hardly available
    Except in the old cook books.

My hair falls asleep
Coiled up beneath
Your hairy armpits
    two atrophied sexes
        from when you were a god.

My hair alone is asleep
It alone slumbers
    Not me!

I keep running and pricking myself
In the thistles violaceous and tiny
    of your breath
In the thistles
    ever resolute
        of your heart's rose
Perceptible
Even in the dark.

Before the break of the day I'll have to reach
The end of the world
    the end of the night
Where the wish
    begins to hurt
And where you dream about awaiting me.

Carolina Ilica • Violet

Where you could get drowned
In the deep of the so-deep lust

Or cut yourself –
        when you let yourself fall down from high up –
In the edge of my scream
        Whose handle is in your hand.

Carolina Ilica • Violet

After A Love Night

Downstairs
      Facing the balcony
Outside my open window
The cherry-tree with red leaves
              in the twilight
Played serenades to me
Or it was you?

Sober
    strong
        intransigent
            concentrated

In the day time
        but quite romantic and full of imagination
In the night
Knowing how to play and take a risk:
      The sword lying between us
           like an armed arm
              A sharp purplish-blue
              border line
      In the middle of the bed
      A cold metallic snake that was lying – it was
      The snake of heaven!
      (Prudence
             temptation
                      and fear?!)
I did not cut myself
      but there was blood flowing.
For the dawn of that day
                following that night
Was heavy
      was red
            as deflorations.

But how free and at ease
              the morning felt like!

Carolina Ilica • Violet

        Stopped
before a tow
           overloaded
with cages:
Doves
    Males
    Females
        (In pairs)
For a pigeon exhibition.

I was winged as they were
After that love night.
And just like you they kept cooing happily.

Carolina Ilica • Violet

Afforestation

I imagine that you suffer from subtle amnesia
Just like the characters in many South American soap operas
That you settle down in such a country
Living in its metropolis
                    lying
In a barren plain
      flat as a hand
             exposed to the winds and the drought
A metropolis
With no parks in it and no forests around it.

So that you can hardly remember anything about the past
And may be chosen by another fate
And may stay
      with another
            Foreign woman.

That I miss you.
But for these reasons
As well as for many others
              subjective / objective.
Why would I write you:
      'I miss you?!'
And then I would draw one tree for you
And another one
      with each letter
And little by little
To forest the sight
Before your window
Around your house
Farther and farther away
To then draw mountains also
      and hills
           and vales
I forest them all:

With Christmas trees.

Carolina Ilica • Violet

With tiny hawthorns
    invaded by the guests
        of the white flowers
            watched over by thorns.
With beeches rustling and long life oaks
With effeminate
    birches.
With alder trees very bitter
    and solitary maples.
With linden trees dreaming
    like poets.
With weeping willows with many shoots
        floating upon the water.
With poplars very upright
    candles reaching the sky
        with leaves in the shape of some hearts
            in fibrillation…

And the forests will grow to teem with
Phreatic springs
And wild animals
Great and free
    magically
        multiplying
As in 'One Hundred Years in Solitude.'
With no fruits on the branches
    But birds
Vividly coloured
That begin singing
And you understand
All they say.

And in the clearings
    in spring
    tenderly trembling
There sprout:
    fragile blue caps
        sprinkled
            with snowdrops among them
    shining white-bluish

Carolina Ilica • Violet

      like snow under the moon.
    Hollowworts irresolute like ephebes
    Violets tender and moist
    And chiefly spring crocuses
        dressed
                in dark violet
  and autumn
  in reluctant violet blue.

And so as time goes on
                to change
The forms of relief of your country
The flora and the fauna
And then the climate
And along with them even the people there
    Especially you
Until you also finally come to understand
The meaning and the oppression of the word LONGING.
And only then you begin feeling like yourself again
And our words
              more vivid than blood
Come to flow through yourself
And you can answer me:

When there are many and many
                  Contemporaries – Billions! –
    who have never met
As if they lived in different times and different worlds
It seems too much
That we both
   have met
      after all,
And paradoxically enough,
   that I am with you
   and you are with me.

Carolina Ilica • Violet

But if you will ever want to pass away
Let me know at once and I will come

At least
   to pass away
      together!

Carolina Ilica • Violet

A Bed Too Narrow

On the longest day of the year
Like a clearing freshly stretched out
All sweet-scented woodruff,
    our Lady's bedstraw

And butterflies mauve
    fond of drinking
        erotomaniacs

Long clearing between two clusters
(Of mulberry trees almost ripe
belonging to no one)
Small as two nights in June
    As two little cushions
    As two dozes

So on the solstice
Baked on the afternoon's kitchen range
Remember the shortest day
On the other
    frosty part
        of the year:
A day cold and narrow
As a bed too narrow
Where two people can't find room to sleep
Or to remain awake
    they can't find room either
Only if they bend
Over
    each other
By turn

Like a guardian angel
Or like a lover
    Kissing high and low
    Being kissed high and low.

Nausea

Nausea latent
         for long.
Growing after a while
As the dough in the hollow of the trough:
    swelling up
    overflowing
    ready to fall down
As happens to expectant mothers
    (at first)
    when they are two months pregnant.

The leavened nausea
    the salty nausea
Makes me see
    and see again
On the screen secret and uncertain of my memory
  A man laughing
  Showing off all of his teeth
  As lions and tigers do
  Happy and strong
  In the morning After
      the embraces
            synchronized
  With each cock-a-doodle-do
  In its ancestral memory.

Salty nausea.
    A sea of salt
Gluey and colourless
And yet, and somehow, a very old bluish-grey
plunging into myself

Like an evil for too much good.

Abundance

I need nothing. It's the height of summer.
On the left:
>   soft garments
>> frivolous mauve in colour
>   passed from cyclamen to blue
>   As worn by
>   *Aquilegia vulgaris*
>   called also the gypsy's flower.

Hardly taken off and dropped in the sand
>   they discharge

The energy of my body.

On the right:
>   obese peaches
>> refreshing

With hard stones getting ever harder
Below the hips overripe for their cores.

I need nothing.
Not even the breeze
>   light at first
>> ever lighter, then
>>> hardly perceptible

Like the breath of a far-off wind
At ease in its sleep
Coming from the lofty mountains with forest lungs.

I need nothing.
Not even the cross of life
A shadow now
On the wall
>   of a mediaeval church.

I need not even loneliness –
>   for too much time
>   it's been boasting
>   about my name!

Carolina Ilica • Violet

I need not even the others' love
Or the supreme freedom
      which
I myself win again
      dreaming
            and dreaming of you
So that I miss not even you any more

While the sea
      at my feet
Moving its waves
      its hips
            its foam

Keeps swinging
      over and over again
            nymphomaniac

Under the August sun
      at noon
            too high up
                 priapic.

Hat Veil

Like a coquette
             with sleek hair
Firmly tied at the back of her head
Come out from other times
             quite mysterious
Enveloped in purplish veils
The morn covered
             her face
With a dewy hat veil.

But that hat veil
Of tulle of spider
With large brilliants of dew
Was real, indeed!
Actually
      you saw it
             yourself.
When I said to you: Look!
You looked at it at once. And you saw it.
And, yet,
How could you say
That it was me who had broken it?
             Me
The only one
Who had noticed it
Who had admired it
And I had wondered at it as before a miracle.

And your eyes
      the only ones
             with which
My eyes
      wished to share
That beauty
      Real
             unreal
                  and ideal!

Carolina Ilica • Violet

Absence

I am and I am not here.
There are many people.
The critics introduce poets and some of their books.
    But from now on they will speak
    Only for themselves. For themselves.

I make my escape
To the left:
Through the high window
      where I can see
A tree that is much higher.
    The part of the trunk with no bark on it
    Looks
    Like the torso of a man twisting
    Naked up to the waist.
    Dressed in a pair of trousers blackish and stiff
    Unbuttoned
    And carelessly
      left down
          on his hips.

To the right:
    On the bedding almost blue
              of the sky
Sprinkled with a little violaceous:
A pillow changed
      too white
          a cloud too light.
    I lay my brow on it
    With half-open eyelids
    Dreaming
      and dreaming
    Who knows how long

Carolina Ilica • Violet

Until your eyes looking into mine
    insistently
        telepathically
Wake me up
        raise me from the dead
Bring me back to the present
        Hic et nunc.
Without knowing where
I'd like to put up for the night.

I am and I am not.
The many make me feel more lonely than before.
    And I escape again
    I abandon myself to day-dreaming
    But you bring me back
        You make me go out
    Of my way
        As from my fate.

Carolina Ilica • Violet

Promise

I dare not speak to you about eternity
When all that I have is so transient
Mainly my body
      my fondled body
Dressed in the most beautiful dress
      tight and warm
      of its white skin.

But
As long as I am fond of you
As long as I keep you
      on the pedestal of my heart
            I'll also adore you:
You'll be the sphinx of my lucidity
And the black Minotaur
   of my
      violet
         subconscious.
You'll be the king of my desires
   ever in obedience to
      your desires
And the god of my soul
   ever young
      quite a child.

And as a god
   I'll take you out of time.

But when you wake up –
   should you ever wake up –
Your life would have already passed!

Carolina Ilica • Violet

Moon

Now a Dacian buckler
Then a Dacian falchion
    Of age-old gold
        Extracted from the eight famous mines
            in the Western Mountains
      Maybe from Roşia Montană
        Brad
            or Abrud
                or Băiţa

Ancient weapons
Of offensive and defensive combat
    Exhibited in turn
    In the transparent shop window of the sky
    On the violet-dark purple cushions of plush
Piese de resistance in the night's museums:
THE MOON –
Now full
Now new.

Its archaical golden sheen (unchanged)
Harmoniously in contrast with
The dark purple almost black
    of the darkness
        renewed night by night

Just as I, blond
Beside you once very dark-haired.
And as
    one of us
        who knows when
        alive and small
Beside the other one
        who knows which one
             dead and grown-up.

Dracula II

Remember?
    Simultaneously:
        Paradise and Inferno.

Me calling your name
    from there
Repeating it
Sending it from within me to you
As if a swarm
    unable to alight
Coming back to me again:
    like an echo
        forever in love with itself.

Remember?
The desperate happiness
And the happy despair
    In my eyes
    In my voice
        calling your name aloud and in a whisper
While you came in
    when you came out
        and came in again
In my soul
Ever virgin
    Of Hymen and Hestia.

O happiness of the unhappy
Your colours
    are violet and black?!

Carolina Ilica • Violet

Remember then the sleep
So little
      only a shade
Dew of sleep at the daybreak
Thin and cold as the first snow
Like the sugar powder
On the layers still hot
Of the bed sheets?

And then
      after sleep
That mark
      on your neck
You have already boasted of
      a little later:
Like a purple stain
Through which your blood
      had tasted me
            when I kissed you.

Remember?
Still remember?

It's enough to remember
And that mark
Will appear on you again
      in the same shape
In the same place
      On your neck
            below your ear
                  above your left clavicle
      Between your carotid and your jugular
Like a vampire seal.

Carolina Ilica •Violet

Torture

What sheer torture for you not to be able to sleep
When actually you go to bed to sleep!
      And your bed clothes with beds
      Of irises wet with your dew
      Not seeming cool
            but ablaze.
But how pleasant it is when this torture overwhelms you
When awake
            you dream and live once more
What was yesterday and what will be tomorrow.

It's over now! But tomorrow
      by daylight
Between his knees squeezing
Your knees ever squeezed will grow smaller:
      two rabbits, white,
      chased and squashed
      into two others
           stout and gray
      frightened by themselves
      and all crouched together.

But how many nights will pass
      and will still pass
Until you grow to make them no longer afraid?

And how many more days
      to tame them?

      to make them let you descend
      to the infernal heaven
      hidden in their Bermuda Angle

Carolina Ilica • Violet

Quarrel

We met quarrelling.

I was dressed in violet
      as if in mourning.
And I went on asserting that the human heart
Was as big as two fists
      and I put my fists together.
You contradicted me by saying that it was as big as a fist
                                                    alone.

But my fists aren't they both
As big
      as the fist of a man?!

And I let you get angry. Besides
'You have not even a heart!' – I said laughing –
'How could you measure what you haven't?!

Out of your senses
      you unbuttoned your shirt
Took my head between your palms as if between some
                                                      claws
And pressed my right ear
      as if a warm cupping glass
Against your left shoulder-blade
And forced me
      to listen
            listen
                  listen

But in cold blood I ignored
The gallop within me: a herd of horses
Escaping from the shed across the fields.

Carolina Ilica • Violet

Love
      little as it may be
Comes from the bottom of one's heart
          but you
      You have not even a heart!

To find it
      I should
          look for it
But not from without to within
      Only from within it!

Carolina Ilica • Violet

Delta

Your absence
   leaves
      your presence
         ever behind.

Suffering from nausea
   like an expectant mother
I can no longer bear the shades of mauve
The hemp smell
   of some exotic fruits,
The too sweet sweetness
      of the tango:

The recurrent
   refrains
      still can
         remind me of you again:

Overflowing
Flooding me
Making me a fertile delta
Heaven for birds and water lilies
Natural
   reservation
      not under preservation:

The more vulnerable before you
The stronger in comparison with all the others:

Like a woman
That is nine years pregnant
   And about to give birth to a baby
         And to give birth to you.

Carolina Ilica • Violet

Ripe Fruits

Like some vividly coloured birds
The ripe fruits
    Stand drowsing
        On the branches
Among the leaves.

There's so much peace
    In them!
So much oblivion in the long run
Between those who once were in love with each other.

    But could I ever forget you
    Undressing me
    Painfully slowly
    Pulling down my violet dress
        tight
            as the snake skin
    My purplish-blue underwear?

    Could you ever forget me
    Unbuttoning your shirt with my teeth
    Taking it off by kisses?

    Undressing
    Each other
    So that we might reach our souls.

    Could we ever forget
    The distich of our breath
    The pleasure of giving pleasure?

And however
Ever since then
It's been so much oblivion
Even between us!

Carolina Ilica •Violet

Even if
   for the present
      there still exists only future
                     Oblivion!

Carolina Ilica • Violet

Nocturnal Rain

Stripped to the waist. Excited
Before the window wide open:
   You bend
       and breathe in
   You draw yourself up
       and breathe out.

The nocturnal rain attracted by you keeps playing:
   It clings to your hair
   Trickles down your brow
   Descends the hard line of your nose
   Into the ditch full of herbs
   Of your upper lip.
   It gathers up
       in your chin dimple.

Then it descends
On your neck, on your shoulders
It makes the stiff hair on your breast coil itself
into a ring round its finger.

It looks for your heart
It looks for your soul
       It fondles you high and low
       (As every woman wishes
       To be fondled high and low).

It thus dresses you in a wet embroidered blouse
Which it alone span, wove, stitched
In one night
A blouse called 'victorious' – when under a spell –
So that it may cool you
               Of myself.

Carolina Ilica • Violet

How faithful the rain is!
It will ever come to the tryst
In my place
Whenever you dream of me
And wake up hectic and alone.

Yes
   It will take my place
            before the window
And in lilac fringes only will it be dressed.

Prudent
   Staying quite far away in the day-time
      and looking indifferent
So as to be much more full of passion
    In the night.

How faithful the rain is!
Swinging
    between the chaste shyness
Of the woman
    fallen in love,
        at the beginning,
     and the shameless sensual pleasures
       of the mistress
           in the end.

Poetic Acuity

So accurately
Did you grasp each line
As if
You alone
   had dictated them to me
              in former times.

As if all my life
I'd worn mauve
As a secret mourning
     waiting for you.

So accurately
Do you grasp all that I write
As if
You were my one and only predestined reader.
I remember:
    In a verse
    about the wind
       I added
              (To put you to the test)
    The epithet 'feline.'
    You said to me: 'It's beautiful
        in itself.
    But quite inappropriate here!'

About an old poem you exclaimed:
      'It's perfect!
    Listening to it
      Oh,
    That I had been
The man
    That
    Came into your dream!'

Carolina Ilica • Violet

So accurately do you grasp all that I write
So much poetic acuity do you have
That I could even pass away –
              In peace:

    Here
          on earth
    There will be someone
    to rewrite
    in violet
    India ink
    All
    That I will keep quiet
            (Below ground)!

Carolina Ilica •Violet

I Feel Like Crying

In midsummer I feel like crying
                for summer as
I feel like crying for myself sometimes
                when you are not with me.
Autumn will come
And our lots
    So far
Will look alien even to us.
Autumn will come again
And you also will feel like dying!

Autumn will come
With whips of rain
With penknives of rime
And drops of rime
        coming down
              ever lower
                      like the quicksilver
                              on the thermometer
                                of the stems
Till they shave the scant beard of the grass
                to reach their roots.

Autumn will come again
And your soul
Will emigrate to mine
Under the Gate of Sighs
    Wasting
        ever more light.

Autumn will come
With chrysanthemums
        That are mauve become dirty
                As the blackberry bloom
And then the large simple chrysanthemums
        Covered with rime
That are sallow mauve
As the dead's bluish lips

Carolina Ilica · Violet

Will smell of embalmed
                      Dead.
But where's the scent
      The last
Under the arm of those dying?!

Autumn will come again
And you'll be taken ill
      you also
                  yes, even you,
For the longest illness in the world,
That was given the shortest name,
That is
    LONGING.

Red Apples (Dracula III)

Like one and only poem by Trakl
    Where
        You can count
        Twenty colours and nuances –
That summer day –
        A wide conjugal bed
        Ever growing narrower
        The more it goes down
            the more it burrows
        Into my visual memory:

Like the mountain flora
        the deep violet
Becomes but a shade
            of pink embracing the blue

Dancing
        On a cave wall.
Only a spot left there
        a gloomy wart
            an ugly ecchymosis
On the serene face of a mirror
        with its cold back
            made of silver.

And the then red
        purple
            of noble descent

A pale vampire
rises now
        staggering
In his humid coffin.
Greedy as a pregnant woman
He covets my apples
Sweet-tart-salty
            and red as blood
Which I taste late at night

Carolina Ilica • Violet

  as meat
    on fasting days.

Indeed,
  my apples are hard
   healthy
     glossy
A sort of mountain red
  rustic
    Blood-red
     maidenly

Not vicious and glassy
  as the vampires' eyes.

Apples so red
  that
    you are seized with a desire
     To eat them
 first
  with your eyes!

Carolina Ilica •Violet

Scraping Up Supper

Scraping up supper
         cold
                 in summer
Consisting of cheese, tomatoes
Fruits refreshing and invigorating
All laid on a lilac tablecloth

Unwillingly,
        I remember you
As another
        exotic fruit
              of mango
                        freshly picked up
Smelling also of cannabis
And overripe in my room
During the night.
Unbearably sweet.
Blind as the blind statues in the parks
And, yet, looking at me stealthily:
        As I took off
        My lilac
              underwear
        To fall asleep naked again
        A woman indeed from without
        But a little girl past retrieval
              from within:

        That refuses to fall asleep
              without tales
                      and unrocked.

Carolina Ilica • Violet

Mourning

As holy
As the silk watery and smooth
Indigo – violet
Lining
The sober robes
      black or white
Of the bishops or the patriarchs
That are bound with a girdle
      also indigo
Are saint
      the Crocuses.

For whom do they ever grow and bloom
In spring and in autumn also?
      in spring they are violently violet
          But in autumn they are a sort of mauve
            self-possessed and holy.

For whom this
      everlasting mourning?

For the one that I was
      without you
Very much as nevermore will I be
      with you
          from now on
Nevermore!

Self-Portrait In Sleep

I sleep between two shoulders
                bare and cold
Half out of their sleep
Like two white stones
                round and stable
Come out from the waters of a river
                roiling.

Between them
        Between them
A stone bigger
              oval
                      moved

Ever hot
My head
        is restless.

Its halo of dreams and reveries
Is half visible
        a rainbow raised up
That consists of thirteen nuances
                of violet:
                from the purplish shading off into black
                      like the rimed plum
            to the purplish-blue melted into white.

The other half throbs magnetically
In the computer of the skies
And searches for you
        high and low
So that it may be crowned
Because you wear
The daemon's black
        Halo.

II.

THE SHORT POEM OF MY LONG LIFE
13 (DOUBLE) POEMS OF LOVE

Translated by Lidia Vianu

1.

a) Woodlander

How I wished I could be like my mother!
Woodland wild being,
With a cub. Centaurs –
Men astraddle – on the lookout to steal her.

Hunters hunting with their eyes!
Sweating like a flower,
She simply pretended not to see them.
She just squeezed my hand harder.

Carolina Ilica • Violet

1.

b) Woodlander

Father, do not strike the horses, never strike
                            the horses again, father!
Their neighing pierces me, flashing like a fillister.
Grown in their mane as long as guilty grass,
I dared cry, childishly cry for the death
                            of snowy newly-weds.

My horses, crazy like myself, my horses
                            running away like my eyes!
The lava of my blood scorches me,
                            snow hard in my hearing!
Let your nostrils thrill the air with pleats of dresses,
Let teeth bite off my hair as maize beards!

Overwhelm the demon web under your hooves,
Steal me into the mane with heaven-like darkness!
Why does father worry now? – I know: he would
                            like to marry me
To a lad more upright than the fir-tree,
                            used to beating horses.

2.

a) Woodlander

My hair is a bridleless colt
On the meadow of the new-moon night.

My body smells like corn-field,
My fresh breath is dew.

With his emperor lust
My blood burns my maidenly inside.

Oh, in the arms of which man
Will I first give out light?!

2.

b) A Dress

An anxious dress
Like a spring crocus:
Violently violet
Inside and outside.

Its cold silk,
Snake-like and pure,
Born, endured
Like a straightjacket

By my hot sinful
Skin.
Both
Smell of myself;

That is, of life
With death inside.
My soul, living bird,
Can you rend them?

3.

a) One Evening

I was sleep's toy:
He put coins on my lids,
      Little coins on my lids
One evening. Outside,

The wind undressed the orchard
Petals like dresses,
      The wind lured the orchard,
Kissing her armpit.

3.

b) Shameful

I caught her one night: shameful
She was secretly kissing an apple on a branch.
      My mouth
      Secretly kissing

An apple high up (I was on tiptoe)
So cold it was, it reminded me
      Of your mouth,
      Your burning mouth.

4.

a) Dream

It felt amazingly good:
A handsome man
Violet eyes, broad chest,
Had entered my dream at night.

What he whispered, it will not do
For me to utter out loud now.
I faced him: Go your way,
I was not waiting for you!

Why do you fight, Pride,
His eyes asked me.

And he laughed, oh, how wildly!

When I woke up, I was scared:
I was burning with lust and pride.

4.

b) Temptation

Attracted by the fresh, white naked body, let him come
A demon in the waters of the mirror: even Satan.
Pull thick curtains, keep light away
The scary laughter and the ugly face.

But when he holds you, more lustful than the gods
The wise ones, purer than
The child suckling the woman's milk,
Do not be bashful, oh, how you lusted for him!

5.

a) He Was Caressing Me

He was caressing me. And his fingers
Were not five,
But six.
Not six,
But seven.
Not only seven,
But eight.
Not merely eight,
But nine.
Not nine,
But ten.
Not ten,
But thirteen!

The pleasure of caressing
Had multiplied his fingers.
The pleasure of being in their power
Made me feel so lonely!

5.

b) Sleepless Nights

Oh, sleepless nights, nights of love,
Below your chest when I give up all of myself.

The air, true cloister,
Lights candles in plum blossoms.

Oh, sleepless, waiting nights,
When I pray to God, Give him to me,

With so much longing and passion,
That drops fall molten onto my forehead.

6.

a) Nightflier

From you to me:
Wolf howl only.

You sniff at the silence that comes and goes
When howls rave howls.

Armpits, remnants of divine sexes,
Hold your own body with them!

6.

b) Nightflier

From me to you:
Bee swarm.

Open your arms to let them nestle!
In the armpits:

Flower wax.
Light it when you feel like dying!

7.

a) Lakes

I was cooling myself after you, with a whole lake,
                                                in summer.
It was not the long, sleek snakes, cautious into evening
That slept, it was lotus flowers with their heads
                                                  above water.

For the first time guilty fish girls
Waved under waves, silvery backs.
Not they, just the fish men jumped far ahead.

Grand sedge kept mirroring itself.
There was no wind, but it shivered like me.
You did not touch me, yet I shivered all the same.

7.

b) Lakes

Like mauve gauze: watery – like
    The silk of a lake.
I was coming in the evening, among the sedge.
    Swim little, keep silent more.

They threw slow rods
    With rough, transitory thread,
Alluring with rustles and whispers
    The undying sky Fish.

But I fell willingly, caught
    In the net of the moon.
As in the arms of the man
    I still longed for.

He seemed a spell all around –
    How could I breathe and not rend it? –
At the nakedness of water, my body
    All ashamed, a child again,

When the lake floated me on its chest
    Like a leafless lotus.
Night, from the skies, enveloped us
    In darkness, both of us.

I felt secure that nobody, no one
    Here, at least, would ambush me.
As we usually think that death
    Will find only the others.

8.

a) "Calea Victoriei"*

Crooked, "Calea Victoriei"
Seen from above. Anthill.
You breathe too closely. You breathe down
My temple, quickly, then calmly.

This burning heat
Softens something in me:
Distance, silence, pride?
The skill, the art to deny?

There is so much sadness in the world!
But sometimes you need
So little, here we are, to forget...
So little, here we are, to die.

* *Old boulevard in the center of Bucharest.*

8.

b) Love

For years I have been a prisoner in your goals,
Love, wild queen!
The flowers of my cheek are pale.
But the longing heart is purer.

I am not strong enough to oppose;
Even if I were, I could not, not openly.
Instead of cursing you and damning,
I praise you, doomed for life.

You play with me in the daytime, you leave me
On my own, a kind of freedom
The large city gives to the crowd.

But at night you chase and lay me down,
Forcing me to please you in everything...
You buy and sell me for a dime.

9.

a) Haystacks

Haystacks, wild, silky breasts; silken
And aromatic. They endure nakedness
Shamelessly; heavy and separated;
Stroked or kissed by nobody.

From another world,
pure and august,
As at the breast of a sinful nurse,
Tiny little stars come: they smell and taste.

9.

b) Snails

They have a softness of the world beginning
And mild vegetal slowness.
When they touch and taste – all at once –
The slimy leaves.

They are primitive. Sensuous. And so
Slowly, voluptuously, shamelessly
They leave and return to crammed shells
As if they were making love to themselves.

10.

a) Exquisitely

Sunken eyes, pale faced,
I was at the window, waiting.
Outside it was raining carefully.

And the rain stuck to the panes.

In your turn, at another window,
You were waiting for somebody else:
Who may have been waiting

For someone who was waiting for me.

The winding chain! Links
Closing in upon one another.
Let us call it exquisitely:

Unrequited love!

10.

b) In Your Eyes

In your eyes am I only
A flower in another flower's shadow?
When the sky is low and grim,
The petals lock themselves in sepals.

If you were to pick me up in your hand,
Like the lotus I should suddenly open:
At first shameless and heathen.
Then heathen and shameless.

11.

a) Out Of Fire And Ice

> Motto:
> *What a pity!*
> *When I am wise enough,*
> *I will not be*
> *Young enough!*

Youth is already slipping and you feel
You have not loved enough.

You touch your forehead: ice on embers.
Out of fire and ice your life
Is made. A double life.

Still looking between lashes? The one
You are watching does not even believe,
Does not believe you could be his alone.
Like an aged eagle, thirsty with hunger,
Doubt in him
Hovers lower, closer, nearer by
He rushes at your lips
Lipsticked all red.

Youth is already slipping away and you know
That you have not loved enough.
Your witnesses could be
The flirting dandelions
And the autumn crocus
Saintly smelling
Can bear witness to that.

11.

b) Summer Wanes

Summer wanes. And you cannot hold it.
How can I hold it, when I cannot stop
You, although I lock you within myself.

Summer wanes. Flowers droop
In sleepy indifference
Not caring any more what they look like.

Summer wanes. Birds shriek
Instead of chirping under the wing.
What was was. Slowly undone

The charm, the languor and the sweetness...
Rains hang about with mist.
Summer wanes. Youth. Life.

12.

a) The Evening-Plane

Silver dragonfly trembling in my ear,
The Evening-Plane.
Smoke, too dense a silence floats
Behind, over the whole city.

I used to wait for the Evening-Plane...

The Museum of Memories preserves
Unhealed details ever since:
A flower crushed by a step. A bee.
A lost child. Dead phones
In the open, strange post office.

I used to run towards Love
In new sandals made of impatience.

I am ashamed now:
I am an old woman who can hardly
Remember myself.

12.

b) In Childhood
(The Master of the World)

The handcuffs of his hands
On my ankles
I can still feel;

Although I am losing the time
When a boy
Strongly grabbed
My small palms –
Two golden epaulets –
Pressed them on my shoulders and shouted:

– I am
The master of the world!

13.

a) The Short Poem Of My Long Life

I do not have the gift of being rich.
Even less that of being happy.
And yet once upon a time
My heart filled up:

Was it love or poetry?
It's all the same! I might as well die.
If I am still alive, it's only to describe
The longing for that longing mood.

13.

b) Like a Peasant

I sowed basil one sacred Friday noon.
Like a peasant.
I watered it with my mouth.
Thinking of God and Love,
As if they were one!

Here it flowers! Here I am
Basil in my breast!
Like a peasant.
Wanted and willing.

Be the first to smell me, my God!

THE TRANSLATORS

Olimpia Iacob, translator and poet, is Associate Professor in Modern Languages at Vasile Goldis West University of Arad, Romania.

Jim Kacian is an American poet, editor, publisher, translator and public speaker. He is the founder of Red Moon Press, and editor of *Frogpond*, the journal of the Haiku Society of America. With Ban'ya Natsuishi and Dimitar Anakiev, Kacian co-founded the World Haiku Association. He also formed and created The Haiku Foundation.

Lidia Vianu, poet, essayist, prose writer, translator, editor, teaches Modern and Contemporary English Literature at the University of Bucharest. She founded the MA Translation Program of the Contemporary Literary Text and is the Director of the online publishing house Contemporary Literature Press. In 2005, she received, with Adam J. Sorkin, the London Poetry Society biennial Prize for Poetry in Translation.

RESPONSE TO CAROLINA ILICA'S WORK

"One of our most talented women-poets – maybe the most gifted of all – Carolina Ilica often manages to change poetry into a kind of erotic magic. Like the snake seduced by the tamer's magic flute, an irresistible sensuality opens like a spiral in the reader's soul (...). The interesting part is that the poetess exerts her seduction lucidly, constantly preserving her sharpness, precision, even surgeon-like cruelty. Like no other poet, Carolina Ilica describes just those scenes which, by their disturbing ambiguity of chastity and guilt, create the highest erotic tension (...) as a matter of fact, Carolina Ilica distinguishes herself by a sort of ambitious hunt for the inexplicable."
—Alex. Ştefănescu, Romania, 1975

ADVANCE RESPONSES TO THE ENGLISH TRANSLATION, *VIOLET*

CAROLINA ILICA presents the English reader with a fine selection of her trademark sensual and melancholy verse that puts love and poetry on a par with each other. Via mythology, nature, seasons and other poets, she links the passion and longing of the past with the reality of today. Ilica's poems are dynamic and alive. She is courageously personal and not afraid to reflect the vulnerability and fleetingness of passion, bringing out feelings that are both strong in their longing and delicate and fragile in their existence. The earthiness of her poems is convincing. Beyond offering verses of sensual experiences and desire, her poems are filled with life, love and vitality that spring from social interaction and deeply felt togetherness – experiences that do not age. Ilica summarizes her poetry in 'The Short Poem of My Long Life': "If I am still alive, it's only to describe/The longing for that longing mood."
—**Birgit Bunzel Linder**
Author of *Shadows in Deferment* (Proverse, 2013, Winner of the Proverse Prize 2012), *Bliss of Bewilderment* (Proverse, 2017)

LIKE THE AIR ROOTS of a thousand banyan trees reaching down to touch the earth, seemingly so is the author's desire for physical love. But her poetry is not really about sex. It is about a human soul finding itself, the purpose of its existence, in the arms, on the chest and other private parts of a man. Sex is only a means and poetry is another for the realisation of her being in her short life on earth. She has obviously succeeded.

The verses of the poems are tense, terse, analytic, capturing the many layers of experience in enlightened sexual acts that we do not yet have the vocabulary for. The spacing of the words is

meticulously planned, allowing for a divergence of meanings that make you blink. A definite clean break from many contemporary poems where form tends to override content, in this work, content dictates and purifies form. As such, Carolina's poetry is one of those works through which we glimpse the minds of the goddesses Aphrodite and Diana – when they hunt down Adonis – if we dare to know the minds of gods at all.
—**Elbert Siu Ping Lee**
Author of *Rain on the Pacific Coast* **(Proverse, 2013)**

THIS WORK is a bramble bush of astonishing twists and thorns, mellifluous with metaphor and inventive simile. It is at once stark and lush, subtle, and emblematic. The medley of violets, mauves, purples and cyclamens creeps through the collection's soul, providing a poetic fest of beautifully inventive and evocative forms.

I find it a sensuous, drench-dipped journey into the art of metaphysical conceit. It whispers of religious symbolism, yet teases with the pure shock of carnal innovation.

I swam in this work, surrendering to sound, sinking into the "happiness of the unhappy", the duality of 'Hymen and Hestia' ('Dracula II'), aware, always, that my expectations would be undercut in stark and dramatic ways, leaving me with intense but mixed emotions.

The book, to use Carolina Ilica's own image, is "Like a spring crocus:/ Violently violet/ Inside and outside."
—**Hayley Ann Solomon**
Author of *Celestial Promise* **(Proverse, 2017, Proverse Supplementary Prize Winner, 2016))**

SOME POETRY AND POETRY COLLECTIONS
Published by Proverse Hong Kong

Alphabet, by Andrew S. Guthrie. 2015.

Astra and Sebastian, by L.W. Illsley. 2011.

Bliss of Bewilderment, by Birgit Bunzel Linder. 2017.

The Burning Lake, by Jonathan Locke Hart. 2016.

Celestial Promise, by Hayley Ann Solomon. 2017.

Chasing light, by Patricia Glinton Meicholas. 2013.

China suite and other poems,
by Gillian Bickley. 2009.

For the record and other poems of Hong Kong,
by Gillian Bickley. 2003.

Frida Kahlo's cry and other poems,
by Laura Solomon. 2015.

Home, away, elsewhere,
by Vaughan Rapatahana. 2011.

Immortelle and bhandaaraa poems,
by Lelawattee Manoo-Rahming. 2011.

In vitro, by Laura Solomon. 2nd ed. 2014.

Irreverent poems for pretentious people,
by Henrik Hoeg. 2016.

The layers between (essays and poems),
by Celia Claase. 2015.

Of leaves & ashes, by Patty Ho. 2016.

Life Lines, by Shahilla Shariff. 2011.

Mingled voices: the international Proverse Poetry Prize anthology 2016,
edited by Gillian and Verner Bickley. 2017.

Mingled voices 2: the international Proverse Poetry Prize anthology 2017,
edited by Gillian and Verner Bickley. 2018.

Moving house and other poems from Hong Kong,
by Gillian Bickley. 2005.

Over the Years: Selected Collected Poems, 1972-2015,
by Gillian Bickley. 2017.

Painting the borrowed house: poems,
by Kate Rogers. 2008.

Perceptions, by Gillian Bickley. 2012.

Rain on the pacific coast,
by Elbert Siu Ping Lee. 2013.

refrain, by Jason S. Polley. 2010.

Shadow play, by James Norcliffe. 2012.

Shadows in deferment, by Birgit Bunzel Linder. 2013.

Shifting sands, by Deepa Vanjani. 2016.

Sightings: a collection of poetry, with an essay, 'communicating poems', by Gillian Bickley. 2007.

Smoked pearl: poems of Hong Kong and beyond,
by Akin Jeje (Akinsola Olufemi Jeje). 2010.

Of symbols misused, by Mary-Jane Newton. 2011.

Unlocking, by Mary-Jane Newton. March 2014.

Wonder, lust & itchy feet, by Sally Dellow. 2011.

THE INTERNATIONAL PROVERSE POETRY PRIZE (SINGLE POEMS)

An annual international poetry prize (for single poems) was established in 2016. The international Proverse Poetry Prize (single poems) is open to all who are at least eighteen years old whatever their residence, nationality or citizenship. Single poems, submitted in English, are invited on (a) <u>any subject or theme, chosen by the writer</u> OR (b) <u>on a subject or theme selected by the organizers each year</u>.

Poems may be in any form, style or genre. Each poem should be no more than 30 lines (not counting the title and blank lines).

Entries should previously be unpublished in any way (except in the case of unpublished translations into English of the entrant's own work already published in another language, providing the entrant holds the copyright).

In 2016-2018 inclusive, cash prizes were offered as follows:
1st prize; USD100.00; 2nd prize: USD45.00;
3rd prizes (up to four winners): USD20.00.

KEY DATES FOR THE PROVERSE POETRY PRIZE IN 2017 ONWARDS
(subject to confirmation and/or change)

Receipt of entered work, entry forms and entry fees	7 May to 30 June of the year of entry
Announcement of Winners	Before April of the year following the year of entry
Cash Awards Made	At the same time as publication of the winning poems (whether in the Proverse newsletter or website, or in an anthology)
Publication of an anthology of winning and other selected entries	Contingent on the quality of entries in any year

The above information is for guidance only.
More information, updated from time to time, is available from the Proverse website: proversepublishing.com

FIND OUT MORE ABOUT OUR AUTHORS, BOOKS, EVENTS AND LITERARY PRIZES

Visit our website: http://www.proversepublishing.com

Visit our distributor's website: www.chineseupress.com

Follow us on Twitter
Follow news and conversation: twitter.com/Proversebooks
OR
Copy and paste the following to your browser window and follow the instructions: https://twitter.com/#!/ProverseBooks

"Like" us on www.facebook.com/ProversePress

Request our free E-Newsletter
Send your request to info@proversepublishing.com.

Availability
Available in Hong Kong and world-wide from our Hong Kong based distributor, The Chinese University of Hong Kong Press, The Chinese University of Hong Kong,
Shatin, NT, Hong Kong SAR, China.
Email: cup-bus@cuhk.edu.hk
Website: www.chineseupress.com.

All titles are available from Proverse Hong Kong,
http://www.proversepublishing.com
and the Proverse Hong Kong UK-based Distributor.

Stock-holding retailers
Hong Kong (CUHKP, Bookazine)
Singapore (Select Books),
Canada (Elizabeth Campbell Books),
Andorra (Llibreria La Puça, La Llibreria).

Orders may be made from bookshops in the UK and elsewhere.

Ebooks
Most of our titles are available also as Ebooks.

www.ingramcontent.com/pod-product-compliance
Lightning Source LLC
Chambersburg PA
CBHW051132160426
43195CB00014B/2447